Expert consultancy provided by Bryony Lanigan
through Royal Observatory Greenwich, UK.

BOXER BOOKS Ltd. and the distinctive Boxer Books logo
are trademarks of Union Square & Co., LLC.
Union Square & Co., LLC, is a subsidiary of Sterling Publishing Co., Inc.

First published in North America in 2025 by Boxer Books Limited.

ISBN 978-1-4547-1237-4

Library of Congress Control Number: 2024943249

For information about custom editions, special sales, and premium
purchases, please contact specialsales@unionsquareandco.com.

Printed in China
Lot #: 10 9 8 7 6 5 4 3 2 1

11/24

unionsquareandco.com

Spring Street™ created by David Bennett
Written by Sasha Morton
Illustrated by Pintachan
Series editor: Leilani Sparrow • Design by Mark Golden
Series consultant: Mary Anne Wolpert, Bank Street College of Education

SPACE
Contents

Spring Street

You, me, and the universe

No one knows how the universe was formed, but it's the biggest thing that we know about. It's almost too big to imagine, but let's give it a try.

We live on Earth, which is one of eight planets that travel around a star we call our Sun, which is HUGE compared to us.

We call this group of planets and the Sun a *solar system.* There are other planets that travel around other stars outside of our solar system.

If Earth were the size of a grain of sand . . . the Sun would be the size of a tennis ball.

Each planet moves on its own special path, which is called an orbit. The planets are MILLIONS of miles away from one another.

Most of the solar system is empty space.

Our solar system sits inside an absolutely massive section of space. This is called a galaxy. Our galaxy is called the Milky Way. Scientists think there could be as many as two TRILLION galaxies. As there are one million millions in a trillion, that number is hard to imagine, isn't it?

The Sun

1 The Sun is a huge ball of gas, so it doesn't have a solid surface.

2 1.3 million planet Earths could fit inside the Sun.

Our Sun is the biggest thing in the solar system. The word *solar* describes things that relate to the Sun. It's more than 100 times wider than Earth—that is almost 865,000 miles (1.4 million km) across.

3 The temperature on the Sun's surface is around 10,000°F (5,500°C). That's very, very hot. Earth's temperature is an average of 59°F (15°C).

4 Our Sun is a star. All stars eventually run out of energy, but the Sun should keep going for around another 5 billion years.

5 It would take 1,200 years for a human to walk around the Sun at an average pace of 6.2 miles (10 km) a day.

1 What is it made of?

3 Temperature

5 Time it would take for a human to walk around the Sun

2 Size

4 Energy

Mercury

1 Mercury is only slightly larger than Earth's Moon.

Mercury

Earth

Moon

2 The Sun would look three times larger if you lived on Mercury, because Mercury is much closer to the Sun than Earth is.

3 Mercury's surface is covered with craters from where chunks of rock and metal have crashed into it.

The four planets nearest to the Sun—Mercury, Venus, Earth, and Mars—are known as rocky planets. They make up the inner solar system. Mercury is the closest planet to the Sun—and the smallest of them all. Mercury is a hot, dry, and dusty planet. It also moves extremely fast. This small planet whizzes all the way around the Sun in just 88 days—four times faster than Earth.

4 Mercury's entire surface has been mapped by robot spacecraft on two special missions. The spacecraft were called *Marina 10* and *Messenger*.

5 Mercury's temperature can drop from very, very hot during the day to very, very cold at night—from 800°F (426°C) to -300°F (-184°C).

6 Sunlight is around seven times brighter on Mercury than on Earth.

7 Although Mercury travels very quickly around the Sun, it spins very slowly on its own axis. An axis is an imaginary line running through the middle of something. So one day on Mercury lasts for 59 Earth days, or almost 8 ½ weeks.

1 Size

3 Craters

5 Temperature

7 Length of a day

2 Relation to Sun

4 Mapping

6 Brightness

Venus

Venus is the hottest planet in our solar system—the temperature can reach 900°F (475°C). That's not as hot as the Sun, but about 15 times hotter than Earth.

2
Venus's atmosphere is hot enough to melt some metals.

3
Venus is sometimes called Earth's twin because they are almost the same size and are made from similar rocky materials.

Venus is another rocky planet. Do you want to know the coolest thing about Venus? Sometimes you can look up at the night sky and see it without needing a telescope. In fact, if you know where to look, you might even be able to see it during the day. That's because it's the brightest natural object in our sky after the Sun and the Moon.

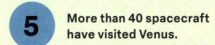

4 Venus is covered with clouds that might smell like rotten eggs.

6 Venus spins clockwise. Earth spins in the opposite direction, counterclockwise.

1 Temperature	**3** What is it made of?	**5** Visitors
2 Atmosphere	**4** Smell	**6** Spin

Earth

1 Earth is the only planet to have just one moon.

2 Earth is the fifth-largest planet in the solar system.

Jupiter

Saturn

Uranus

Neptune

Earth

3 There are 93 million miles (almost 150 million km) between the Sun and Earth. That's the same distance as walking all the way around Earth 3,735 times.

4 It takes 365.25 days for our planet to travel all the way around the Sun once. This is why we have 365 days in a normal year, and 366 days in a leap year. Leap years occur every four years.

Earth is the third-closest planet to the Sun. Scientists say it is in the "Goldilocks zone" because it is not too hot and not too cold. (Just like the porridge in the story "Goldilocks and the Three Bears.") A mission to find more Goldilocks planets is happening right now. Maybe in the future, we'll discover another planet that is just like ours and revolves around a star that gives it just the right amount of heat.

5 A satellite is an object that moves around a larger object. NASA has sent human-made satellites into space to send and receive information from Earth. There are around 9,000 satellites in space above Earth, and this number is growing.

6 Water covers around two-thirds of our planet's surface.

7 The atmosphere (the layer of gases surrounding Earth) is just the right mixture of gases for us to breathe.

8 A day on Earth lasts 24 hours, which is the amount of time it takes our Earth to spin on its axis.

1 Number of moons

2 Size

3 Distance to the Sun

4 A year on Earth

5 Satellites

6 Water

7 Atmosphere

8 Length of a day

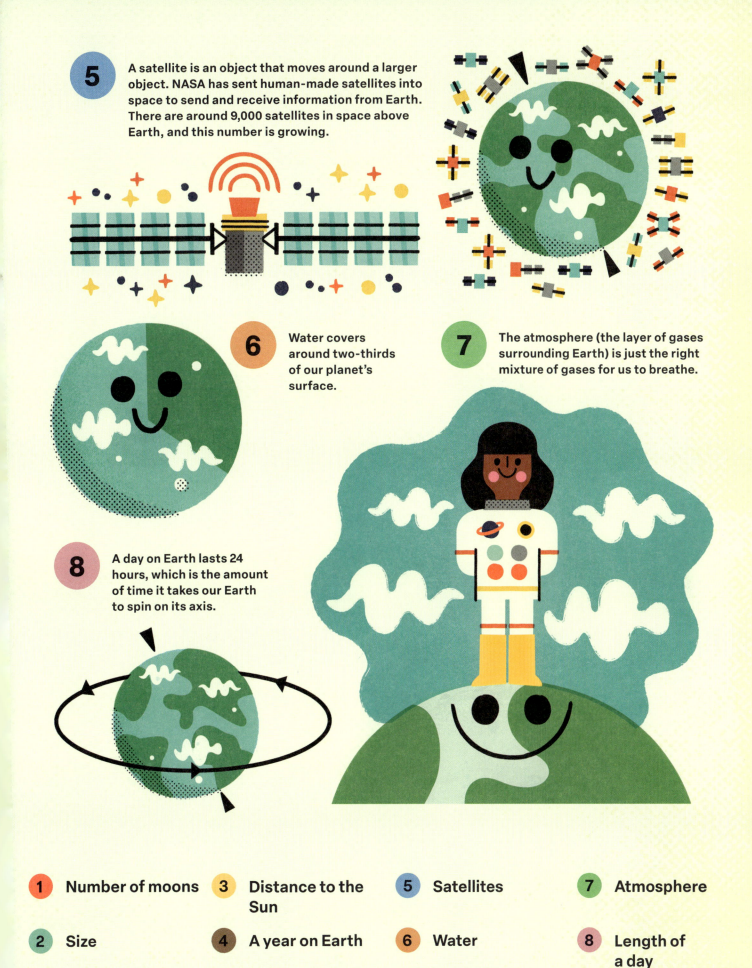

Mars

1 Days on Mars or Martian days are called *sols*.

2 Mars has two moons that look a bit like potatoes. They are called Phobos and Deimos.

3 It takes 13 minutes for sunlight to travel from the Sun to Mars. This is five minutes longer than it takes for sunlight to travel to Earth. This is because Mars is farther away.

Mars is sometimes called the Red Planet because the rusty iron in the ground makes it look red. It's a cold desert planet that is half the size of Earth. Mars has volcanoes, canyons, polar ice caps, and seasons—just like Earth does, but Mars's volcanoes are now extinct. Long ago, it also had water. We know a lot about Mars because it's the only planet where remote-controlled space vehicles have been sent to explore.

4 The two most famous Mars rovers are called *Spirit* and *Opportunity*. They found out that Mars used to have lakes, seas, rivers, and water on the surface and underground.

5 The air on Mars is too thin for humans to breathe, so future astronauts would have to carry oxygen to keep them alive.

6 The largest volcano in the solar system is on Mars—it's three times taller than Mount Everest.

1 Days

2 Number of moons

3 Sunlight

4 Water

5 Air

6 Volcano

Jupiter

1 Jupiter is part of the outer solar system, along with Saturn, Neptune, and Uranus.

Neptune

Uranus

Saturn

2 One year on Jupiter is the same as about 12 years on Earth.

Jupiter is the largest planet in the solar system and one of the brightest objects we can see in the night sky. It is named after the king of the ancient Roman gods who was god of thunder and sky. Jupiter is called a gas giant because it is made up of swirling gases, so it doesn't have a solid surface.

3

An enormous storm has been taking place on Jupiter for at least 200 years, perhaps even longer! It's called the Great Red Spot.

4

Jupiter is 11 times wider than Earth. That's the same as the width of a grape compared to a basketball. 1,300 Earths could fit inside Jupiter.

5

If a spacecraft tried to fly through this gaseous planet, it would be vaporized—that means it would turn into gas and disappear.

6

Jupiter has at least 95 moons and some of them are called . . .

Callisto

Ganymede

Europa

Io

1 Outer solar system

2 Length of a year

3 Great Red Spot

4 Size

5 Flying through Jupiter

6 Number of moons

Saturn

1 Saturn is the second largest planet in our solar system, but despite being massive it would float in water.

2 Because of the way it tilts toward the Sun, Saturn has four seasons—just like Earth. Seasons have different weather and a different number of daylight hours.

3 Around 764 Earths could fit inside Saturn.

Spring

Summer

Fall

Winter

Like Jupiter, Saturn is a gas giant, but it looks different from any other planet because of its amazing rings. All gas giants actually have rings, it's just that Saturn's are the most visible. These rings are made up of billions of tiny pieces of ice and rock. Some seem as tiny as specks of dust, others are the size of a house, and a few are as big as mountains.

4 Saturn has at least 146 moons—more than any other planet.

5 One day on Saturn lasts for 10 hours and 33 minutes.

6 Saturn has seven main rings, which orbit the planet at different speeds.

1 Size

2 Seasons

3 Size in relation to Earth

4 Number of moons

5 Length of a day

6 Rings

Uranus

1 *Voyager 2* is the only spacecraft that has traveled close to Uranus.

2 One year on Uranus is the same as 84 years on Earth.

Uranus has the coldest temperature EVER recorded in our solar system: -371°F (-224°C). This is a surprise, as it is not the planet that is farthest from the Sun. Uranus and Neptune are both known as ice giants and have no solid surface. There is no chance that human or animal life could survive on either of these cold, dark, and windy planets.

3 Uranus is the only planet that rotates on its side.

4 Uranus is named after the Greek god of the sky. It is the only planet named after a Greek rather than a Roman god.

5 No spacecraft could land on the planet's surface, as it is made up of swirling, icy gases.

6 Uranus has 13 rings and at least 28 moons.

1 *Voyager 2*	**3** Spin	**5** What is it made of?
2 Length of a year	**4** Name	**6** Rings and moons

Neptune

1 You could fit 57 Earths inside Neptune.

2 The average temperature on Neptune is -353°F (-214°C). Brrr!

Neptune is almost 2.8 BILLION miles (4.5 billion km) from the Sun, which means it's very cold and dark. Sunlight is 900 times stronger on Earth than it is on Neptune. It has supersonic winds—meaning they travel faster than the speed of sound. Because it's the farthest planet from the Sun, it takes the longest time to travel around it. A year on Neptune lasts for 165 Earth years. That's a long time to wait for a birthday!

3 There are at least 16 moons orbiting Neptune.

4 Neptune is named after the Roman god of the sea.

5 A huge spinning storm on Neptune called the Great Dark Spot was first seen in 1989.

6 Neptune's blue color comes from a gas called methane.

1 Size

2 Temperature

3 Number of moons

4 Name

5 Great Dark Spot

6 Color

25

Space rocks

1 **Comets** are large, frozen chunks of ice and rock that are like giant snowballs orbiting the Sun! They can be seen from Earth as they zoom across the night sky. Some comets can be seen approximately every five to ten years, some are only seen once or twice a century, while others only ever come near the Earth once and never return.

2 **Meteors** are also known as shooting stars. They are the bright streaks we see in the sky when the smallest space rocks, called meteoroids, burn up inside Earth's atmosphere.

It's not just planets that are found in our solar system. There are also too many space rocks to count. Some are hundreds of miles wide and some look like dust. If they were all joined together, they'd still only be the size of our Moon. **But which space rock is which?**

3 **Meteorites** are chunks of rock that make it through Earth's atmosphere and hit the ground.

4 **Asteroids** are lumps of rock left over from when our solar system formed. The area of space where most of the asteroids are is called an asteroid belt.

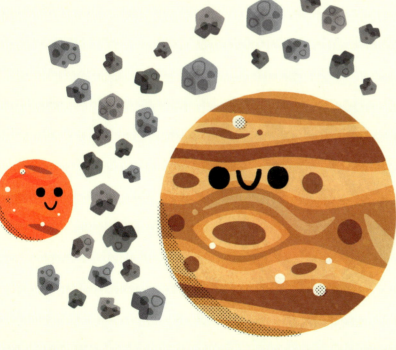

5 The largest asteroids are also known as planetoids.

1 Comets

3 Meteorites

5 Planetoids

2 Meteors

4 Asteroids

Moons and dwarf planets

1 The word *lunar* describes things that relate to the Moon.

2 Gravity from the Moon (or the pull toward its center) is what gives us our tides. It controls the way our water moves on Earth.

3 Scientists think our Moon was made from rocks thrown from Earth after a planet-size asteroid hit it, many billions of years ago.

4 Titan is a moon that orbits Saturn and is the only moon in our solar system to have clouds, and lakes and seas of liquid gas.

Look up at the night sky, and the biggest and brightest thing you can see is our Moon. During the time Earth is orbiting the Sun, the Moon is also going around Earth. Did you know that moonlight is actually just sunlight reflecting off the Moon's silvery surface? Even though it sometimes looks round and other times it is just a thin curve, the Moon never changes shape. We just see different amounts of moonlight depending on the time of the month.

5 A dwarf planet is a planet that doesn't have enough power to shift space rocks or other bits of floating trash out of its way while it orbits the Sun.

6 Each of the five dwarf planets in our solar system is smaller than Earth's Moon.

Moon   Pluto   Eris   Haumea   Makemake   Ceres

7 Pluto used to be known as the ninth planet in our solar system, but in 2006, the International Astronomical Union (IAU) decided it was actually a dwarf planet.

8 Ceres is the closest dwarf planet to Earth—it can be found in the asteroid belt between Mars and Jupiter.

1 Meaning of *lunar*

2 Water

3 Origin

4 Titan

5 Dwarf planet

6 Size of dwarf planets

7 Pluto

8 Ceres

The Kuiper Belt and beyond

The solar system is surrounded by a doughnut-shaped ring of ice and rock called the Kuiper Belt (say *KY-per*), which was left over from when the planets were formed. The Kuiper Belt is on the very edge of our solar system.

1 Objects in the Kuiper Belt are called Kuiper Belt objects, or KBOs.

2 The dwarf planet Pluto is the most famous KBO.

3 A space probe called *New Horizons* has been exploring this part of space since 2006. It took nine years to arrive at an object called Arrokoth in the Kuiper Belt! That's the farthest thing from Earth to ever be explored up close.

 4 Beyond the Kuiper Belt is a swirling shell of icy bits and pieces (and some comets) left over from when the planets were formed. This is called the Oort Cloud.

1 Kuiper Belt objects

2 Most famous KBO

3 *New Horizons* space probe

4 Oort Cloud

Stars and black holes

1 Blue stars are the hottest and biggest stars.

2 Red stars are the coolest stars and can be tiny or gigantic.

3 Some patterns of stars are called constellations. Look out for Ursa Major, also known as the Great Bear, and its smaller section, called the Big Dipper, or for Orion the hunter, next time there are clear skies at night. It is best to look for Orion in the winter as it is not visible in the summer.

Big Dipper

Orion

4 Stars can live for millions or billions of years. They change in size and temperature over this time. Eventually, they run out of power. When a large star dies, it explodes—this is called a supernova.

We have one star in our solar system, the Sun. There are millions of stars living outside our solar system. Stars are huge balls of gas that give off heat and light. They are made when dust and gases spin together inside space clouds. Eventually, these space clouds are dense enough and hot enough to form a glowing star that creates its own light. Hundreds of thousands of stars can be born from one cloud.

5 A black hole is left behind when a really massive star, many times larger than our Sun, dies. This is a place in space where not even light can be seen. Nothing can escape once it enters a black hole.

6 Right now, our Sun is a yellow dwarf star. Before it dies, it will become a red giant. That means it will be bigger—but cooler—than it is now.

7 The most common type of star in the Milky Way is the red dwarf star. These stars can be found all over the galaxy.

1 Blue stars

3 Constellations

5 Black holes

7 Red dwarf stars

2 Red stars

4 Life of a star

6 Our Sun

All about astronomy

1

In Greek, the word *telescopos* means "farseeing," which is a good way to describe what this special piece of equipment does.

2

In 1990, the Hubble Space Telescope was launched to take photographs of planets, stars, and galaxies.

3

A telescope can use magnifying glass lenses and mirrors to collect light and make things that are far away seem closer.

How do we know so much about what is going on millions and billions of miles above our heads? It's all thanks to people called astronomers. Astronomers are scientists who study the universe. They may focus on the Sun, the stars, or the planets—or look for alien life. They can study the skies through telescopes. NASA (National Aeronautics and Space Administration), in the US, and the European Space Agency (ESA) have sent amazing telescopes into space itself.

4

The James Webb Space Telescope was launched in 2021 and is like a time machine. It can collect information about the universe from 13.5 billion years ago.

5

The sky looks different from different places, so we need to have lots of different telescopes around the world. There are huge powerful telescopes in places like Antarctica, China, Chile, and Australia.

1 What does *telescope* mean?

2 Hubble Space Telescope

3 What does a telescope do?

4 James Webb Space Telescope

5 Where are telescopes?

Space exploration

1 The first person to be sent into space was Yuri Gagarin, a Russian astronaut, in 1961.

3 The *Voyager 1* and *Voyager 2* space probes were launched in 1977 to explore interstellar space (beyond the edge of our solar system). They are still gathering information from inside the Milky Way galaxy, which is outside our solar system.

CCCP

1961   1969   1977   1981

2 In 1969, the American astronaut Neil Armstrong was the first man on the Moon.

4 NASA launched 135 space shuttle missions between 1981 and 2011.

We've been making exciting discoveries about our planet and the solar system from the first satellite launch in 1957. Since then, people, telescopes, and spacecraft have gone out into the universe and there is a lot more thrilling space exploration planned for the future.

5 The first space walk where the astronaut wasn't connected to the spacecraft by a cable happened in 1984.

7 In 2009, the Kepler telescope was launched to look for Earth-like exoplanets. Exoplanets are planets in the Milky Way galaxy that orbit stars that aren't our Sun.

9 In 2014, the European space probe *Rosetta* entered the orbit of a comet and sent a lander called *Philae* to its surface!

1984 **1995** **2009** **2011** **2014**

6 Since 1995, the SOHO (Solar and Heliospheric Observatory) mission has been studying the Sun and space weather. The observatory is in space, 932,000 miles (1.5 million km) from Earth.

8 In 2011, NASA's *Dawn* space probe became the first spacecraft to orbit an asteroid.

1 First person in space

4 Space missions

6 SOHO

8 *Dawn* space probe

2 First man on the Moon

5 First unconnected space walk

7 Kepler telescope

9 *Rosetta* space probe

3 *Voyager 1* and *Voyager 2*

More space exploration

1 In 2015, lettuce was the first food to be eaten that had grown in space.

3 The first-ever photograph of a black hole was taken in 2019.

2015 **2018** **2019** **2021**

2 Since 2018, the TESS satellite has been collecting information about the 200,000 nearest stars to Earth. It is also looking for exoplanets.

4 The first-ever sounds recorded on Mars were sent back to Earth in 2021.

5 In 2023, NASA collected the first-ever sample of asteroid dust and landed it on Earth.

7 In 2025, it is planned that the manned spacecraft *Artemis II* will start testing human travel to the Moon before *Artemis III*'s planned launch in 2026.

9 *Artemis IV* is due to lift off into space in 2028.

2023 **2023** **2025** **2027** **2028**

6 The *Europa Clipper* was launched in 2023. It is planned to reach the Europa moon of Jupiter in 2030.

8 From 2027, the *Perseverance* rover will work with a lander and an orbiter to send samples back to Earth from Mars.

1 First food grown in space

2 TESS satellite

3 Photo of black hole

4 Sounds on Mars

5 Sample of asteroid dust

6 *Europa Clipper*

7 Travel to the Moon

8 *Perseverance rover*

9 *Artemis IV*

Space missions

1 Since 2000, seven people at a time have lived and worked on the International Space Station (ISS), which orbits Earth once every 90 minutes. A total of 279 people from 22 different countries have visited the ISS.

2 Each astronaut stays on board for around six months to carry out scientific experiments—some of these can only be done in space.

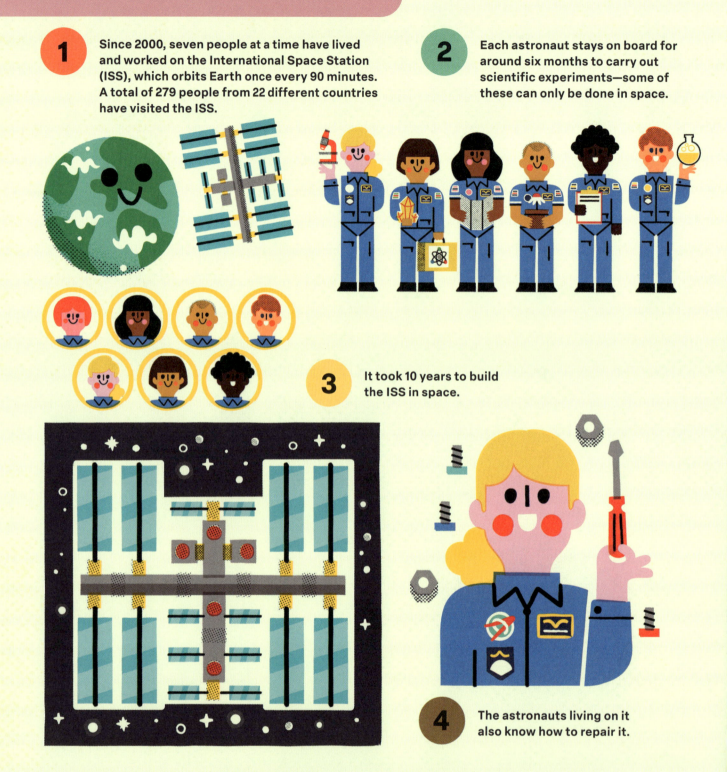

3 It took 10 years to build the ISS in space.

4 The astronauts living on it also know how to repair it.

Space missions are the projects that go into space. Clever technology means that lots of things can be done without people, which is good if a mission is going to take many years to complete! The longest amount of time one person has spent in space is 437 days, on the Russian Mir space station. **How long do you think you could spend in space?**

5 A space station called Gateway (or Lunar Gateway) is due to be built above the Moon to carry out lunar research.

6 Gateway will be the base for the Artemis missions, which will put astronauts on the Moon for the first time since 1972.

8 Astronauts use a specially designed vacuum toilet in space, which stops anything from escaping and floating around the spaceship.

7 One of the main planned Artemis missions is to explore the Moon's South Pole.

9 In space, pee is recycled into clean, drinkable water.

---

1 Number of people on ISS

4 ISS repairs

6 Astronauts on the Moon

8 Going to the toilet

2 How long do they spend in space?

5 Gateway

7 Exploring the Moon's South Pole

9 Recycling pee

3 How long did ISS take to build?

Be a space tourist!

1 Orbital space travel involves traveling at a super-fast speed—around 17,400 miles per hour (27,840 km/hr)—on an orbit around Earth. Imagine what you could see from space!

2 In sub-orbital space travel, a rocket travels straight up, around 62 miles (100 km) above Earth, and back down again. This lets people discover what it's like to feel weightless and "float" in midair for a few minutes when the rocket reaches its highest point.

It takes a long time and a lot of hard work to become an astronaut. Maybe you would like to be a space tourist instead? It's a quicker way to get into orbit, but it will cost you a LOT of money.
Which type of space tourism would you like to try in the future?

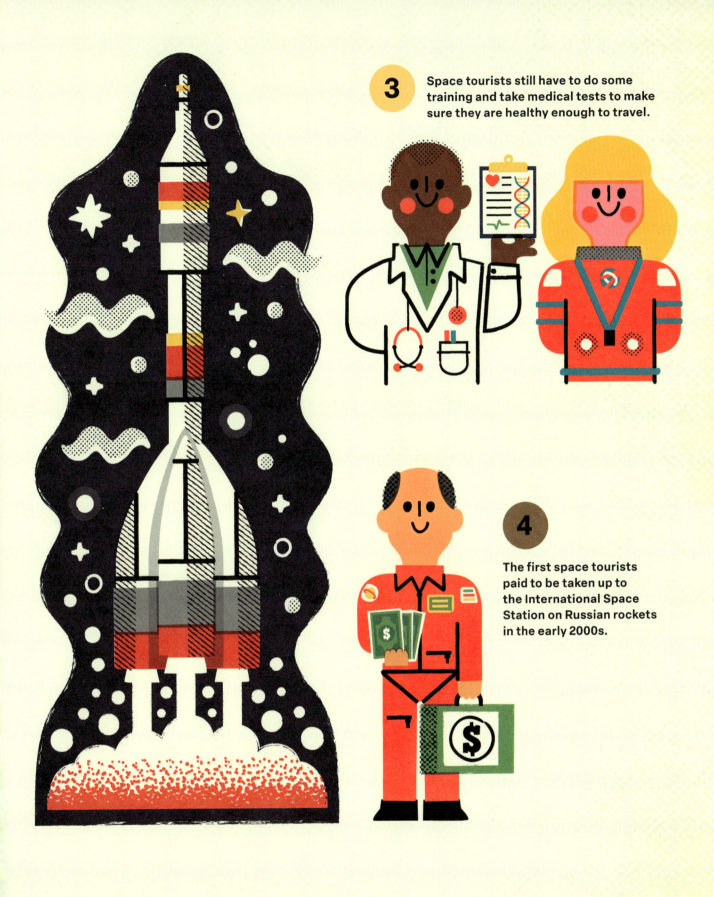

3 Space tourists still have to do some training and take medical tests to make sure they are healthy enough to travel.

4 The first space tourists paid to be taken up to the International Space Station on Russian rockets in the early 2000s.

1 Speed   **2** Weightlessness   **3** Training   **4** First space tourists

A home in space

1 Water: Without water, humans won't be able to survive, so any planet where we try to make our home will need oceans.

2 Transportation: We'll have to develop a way to travel near the speed of light to get to a new planet within our lifetime.

When space scientists working on NASA's Kepler space telescope project started looking for planets that humans might eventually make their home, they realized that there are more planets in the night sky than there are stars. Surely, one of these must be suitable for you and me to live on. After all, there are plans for humans to live on Mars within the next 30 years. **But what would we need to live on another planet?**

3 The right temperature: Our new planet home would have to be not too hot and not too cold.

4 Technology: Spacesuits, ways to send messages home, power . . . all of these need to be safer, faster, and stronger to survive traveling across the galaxy.

Would YOU like to make your home in space?

1 Water   **2** Transportation   **3** Temperature   **4** Technology

Glossary

Asteroid belt—an area of space that contains small rocks that go around the Sun

Atmosphere—a mixture of gases that surrounds a planet

Axis—an imaginary line around which something rotates

Black hole—an area from which nothing can escape

Constellation—a group of stars in the sky that has been given a name because they look like a particular shape

Dwarf planet—small, round object that orbits the Sun, but is not a planet

ESA—European Space Agency

Exoplanets—a planet that orbits a star outside our solar system

Galaxy—a huge collection of dust, gas, and stars and their solar systems

Gravity—an invisible force that pulls objects toward each other

Goldilocks zone—the area around a star where it is possible for a planet like our Earth, suitable for humans to live on, to form

Lunar—to do with the Moon

Martian—to do with Mars

Meteoroids—a small lump of rock or iron that goes around the Sun

Milky Way—the name of our galaxy

NASA—National Aeronautics and Space Administration

Orbit—the curved path around an object in space

Rover—a small mobile robot that is used to explore moons and planets landing on their surface and collecting data

Satellite—an object that orbits a planet or a star

Solar system—a system of a sun and the objects that move around it

Sol—a unit to measure time on Mars; short for "solar day"

Space probe—an unmanned craft sent into space to do research

Supernova—an exploding star

Voyager 1—a space probe launched by NASA on September 5, 1977

Voyager 2—a space probe launched by NASA on August 20, 1977